MUIRFIELD

Sandy Lyle
with Bob Ferrier

World's Work Ltd

First published 1982 by
World's Work Ltd
The Windmill Press
Kingswood, Tadworth, Surrey

Paintings by Ken Turner
Photography by David Pocknell

Copyright © Lennard Books Ltd 1982

SBN 437 09062 0

Made by Lennard Books
The Old School
Wheathampstead, Herts AL4 8AN

Editor Michael Leitch
Designed by David Pocknell's Company Ltd
Production Reynolds Clark Associates Ltd
Printed and bound in Belgium by
Henri Proost & Cie, Turnhout

Back cover photograph by
Lawrence Levy

MUIRFIELD

Muirfield

'The Honourable Company of Edinburgh Golfers' – what a marvellous title, with a grand medieval ring to it. Such grandeur is appropriate, because the Honourable Company, which owns the course at Muirfield, played a critical part in the creation of golf as an organized sport, and is generally accepted as the oldest golf club in the world, dating from 1744.

Perhaps inevitably, the Scots being as they are, this is disputed, principally perhaps by the Royal Burgess club on the other side of Edinburgh, but on the basis of continuously documented records the claim of the Hon Coy is sound. It was in existence ten years before the Royal and Ancient, and the Society of St Andrews Golfers.

A spectacular part of the course considered by many to be the finest championship course in Britain

Introduction

What the Hon Coy did beyond any dispute was to formulate the first regulations for playing the game, now widely known as 'The 13 Articles'. This 1744 code was adopted almost word for word when St Andrews drew up its rules a decade later, and they still form the basis of the present body of rules.

So when you step into the spacious, comfortable clubhouse at Muirfield, you step into golfing history. The solid red sandstone encloses centuries of golfing memorabilia, including portraits of past captains (and powerful Scottish personalities they all seem to have been), plans of the evolution of the course, and the club's fine old silver.

Like all such aged institutions, the club has seen good times and bad, has been rich and poor. It started when 'several Gentlemen of Honour, skilful in the ancient and healthful exercise of golf' petitioned the City of Edinburgh to provide a silver club for annual competition on the links of Leith (five holes) in the spring of 1744. To their credit the City Fathers obliged, and the 4th 'silver club' was presented to the club in 1980.

By 1836, the links of Leith, which were public land, had become too crowded and the club moved to Musselburgh. In 1891 it moved further away from Edinburgh to a piece of ground near Gullane which Andrew Kirkcaldy, as caustic of tongue as he was skilled at 'the golf', dubbed 'an auld watter meadie' (an old water meadow). With

the spread of the railway system came a branch line to Gullane, leaving a stroll of some three-quarters of a mile to the course, and the members were able to disregard the distance from Edinburgh. Only one year later, they were able to stage an Open Championship, won by Harold Hilton.

'Bench and bar' were strongly represented in the membership in the early years; the notables of Scottish law are much in evidence in the original records, and that trend persists. The club has always favoured matches and wagers, holding that the man-to-man match, or at least foursomes play, is the true essence of the game. The Hon Coy does not much fancy par and bogey, it has no need for a professional or professional's shop, using instead the services of the professional from neighbouring Gullane.

The course itself is something of a marvel. When you stand in front of the clubhouse, the property lies before you in splendour – spacious yet strangely private, with everything open to be seen. It is all very different from the King's Course at Gleneagles, where every fairway is secluded from its neighbour. Save for a few houses set well back from the first fairway, on the left side, the course is not overlooked at any point. With Portmarnock (1893), it was one of the earliest courses in the world to use the design concept of two loops of nine, running contra to each other. Muirfield is clearly the gem of that wondrous East Lothian golfing coast, and many eminent golfers, not the least of them Jack Nicklaus, hold it to be the best and fairest test of all the championship courses of these islands.

If there is one outstanding feature of this course, it is the bunkering. The three par-five holes are quite magnificent. There is a healthy blending of long and medium par fours and all the short holes are testing. Everywhere the bunkering is subtle, devious, menacing, and often quite penal.

In the driving zones, and in the angles of the dog-leg holes, the bunkers compromise the drives quite specifically. It is a platitude to say that to play well you

THE HONOURABLE COMPANY OF EDINBURGH GOLFERS

MUIRFIELD CHAMPIONSHIP TEES

hole	metres	yards	score
1	411	449	
2	319	349	
3	346	379	
4	165	181	
5	510	558	
6	431	471	
7	169	185	
8	406	444	
9	452	495	
OUT	3209	3511	

hole	metres	yards	score
10	434	475	
11	353	386	
12	348	381	
13	140	153	
14	409	447	
15	362	396	
16	172	188	
17	496	542	
18	409	447	
IN	3123	3415	
OUT	3209	3511	
TOTAL	6332	6926	

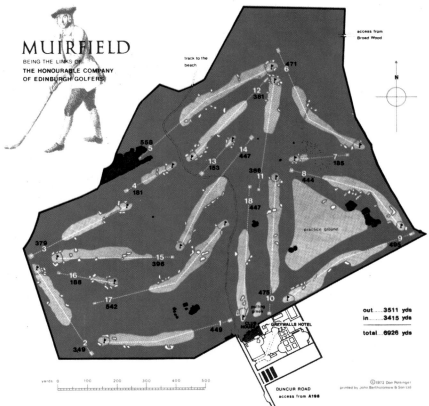

MUIRFIELD

BEING THE LINKS OF
THE HONOURABLE COMPANY
OF EDINBURGH GOLFERS

out......3511 yds
in.........3415 yds

total...6926 yds

must drive well – that should apply to every golf course. But at Muirfield there are none of the margins which you might find at St Andrews or even occasionally at Carnoustie. Muirfield is a driver's course. They say that Henry Cotton, in winning the 1948 Open Championship, missed

Left: A view inland and to the south

only four fairways in 72 holes, and Jack Nicklaus in 1966 seldom used a driver in order to hold his shot in prescribed positions. The greenside bunkering and complementary slopes are major hazards at Muirfield, and one characteristic which should be early apparent is the pair of fairway

bunkers, placed anywhere from 30 to 80 yards short of the green, used on so many holes.

Muirfield is hallowed ground as much as is St Andrews. It has produced such Open Champions as Vardon, Braid, Hagen, Cotton, Player, Nicklaus, Trevino and Watson. Yet for the average player,

playing from the medal tees, there is great pleasure and a good deal of success to be found. No water, no trees, no crippling carries – the course is fair and open to all who play sensibly and well, and who bring to it the respect it merits and demands.

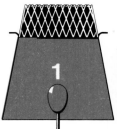

1

444YDS 406M
PAR 4

The long bunker at the front right of the green threatens any approach from that side

This is the most difficult opening hole of any of the great Scottish links courses, a very severe test which only underlines the fact that you should be properly warmed up before you tackle Muirfield. The hole is flat, running to the west, and the fairway is narrow. There is a very large C-shaped bunker to the left, on the edge of the fairway, extending from 202 to 230 yards out from the tee. You cannot quite see all of it from the tee, but it is quite driveable for the average player, and into a strong wind would still be in play for the professionals.

Thus the drive is tricky. The hole seems to tend to the left, then angles back slightly to the right. The actual teeing ground gives the impression of being aimed to the right of the line, so make quite sure of your alignment – it is very easy to aim off to the right without quite realizing it, and be in the rough. Check the quality of that rough – there are no bunkers on the right side of this fairway, and if the rough is light, it is better to be there than in that left-hand bunker. If you are in the

Two bunkers in the short rough

Large bunker at 200–230 yards must be avoided at all costs

2nd shot at the 1st

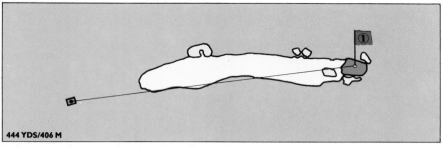

444 YDS/406 M

bunker, you are dead in terms of making any kind of score on this hole, so, ideally, be in the fairway to the right of it. Beyond the bunker, the fairway narrows. The further you drive, the narrower the fairway becomes until, at about 300 yards, it broadens again.

No matter how well the average player drives, he will be facing a long and difficult second shot. Against a rather strong wind, I have hit two of my best shots and still not reached the green. The back point of that bunker is 186 yards from the front of the green, so

if you have driven that far, you may well be 210 yards from the flag. The second shot, all things considered, is possibly even more complex. There are two bunkers in tandem up on the left, only just in the rough, about 90 yards from the middle of the green. Again, you may not see them clearly from the position of your drive. There is a long, rather than a cross, bunker short of the green which rather blocks off the right half of it. There are greenside bunkers along the right side, and at the back left. Thus the left-

front quarter of the green is open, and that should be your way in – precisely why these two bunkers are placed where they are at the edge of the rough, short left, to check people from going wide to the left to open up the green even more.

This first hole is a perfect illustration of the point-to-point nature of the game of golf, and quite obviously demands very careful positional play. Ideally your second shot should pass right of the two bunkers in the left rough, but at the same time stay to the left of that long fairway

bunker. If you are not quite sure of making the distance, aim at that fairway bunker and stay short of it.

This may indeed be your best plan. You must accept that this is a difficult hole, and the average player would do well to play it as a par 5. Being short of the fairway bunker will leave you a tidy pitch to the centre of the green, which is reasonably flat, sloping only slightly left to right, and if you score five on the hole, do not fret – you can be well content with that.

Left front of the green is the best target area

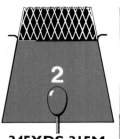

345YDS 315M PAR 4

At first glance, after the rigours of the first hole, this one looks like a catch-your-breath hole, an innocent, perhaps even a birdie hole, but beware. It does not play quite as easily as it looks. The hole runs almost due north-west, and your first task, as ever, is to get the ball on the fairway. It does look inviting. This fairway is broad, but rather undulating and in the driving zone will be inclined to turn the ball from right to left, and much of it slopes downhill, throwing the ball forward.

The drive may bring into play a variety of traps. There is a bunker in the right rough at about 160 yards, innocent enough. A little past the 200-yard mark a pair of bunkers straddles the fairway, one on either side, just in the rough. Plenty of room between them. The backs of these are 100 yards from the front of the green, so if you are in the fairway level with them, or just past them, you should have a pitch-type shot to the green. There is yet another bunker on the

Above:
The broad fairway sloping downhill most of the way

Out-of-bounds wall comes close to the left side of the putting surface

2nd shot at the 2nd

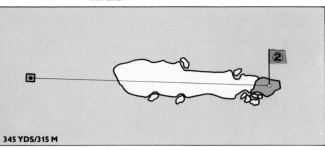

345 YDS/315 M

left side, almost 300 yards from the tee; who knows, in very dry conditions, downwind, pitching your absolutely best drive on a down-slope, you could just

reach it. In these circumstances, many professionals would use an iron from the tee for accuracy and the precise length they wanted. The rough, particularly on the right side, is usually quite strong on this hole.

The approach shot is rather less easy than it may seem. You will not get any particular hold on this green, since the landing zone on the front part of the green slopes downhill, away from you. It might make sense to drive a shade short on this hole, taking a line five yards inside the right-hand bunker, giving

yourself a full shot at the green, rather than a half or three-quarter shot. This gives you a better chance of getting more control on the ball.

There is an army of bunkers by the green – five of them, in varying sizes, all to the right. To the left of the green, a stone wall, which marks the out-of-bounds along the whole left side of this hole, angles in quite close to the putting surface, with only a few feet of fringe between. The green, although quite strongly contoured, is very large, and you should not have major

problems in hitting and holding it. There is no reason to think that you cannot make par here – and optimists have little reason not to think of a possible birdie. One factor to consider, however, is that you may not be fully into your stride, may not be warmed up properly, may be still a little stiff. This is reason again to stress the need to prepare well on the practice ground, and to concen-trate extra hard over the opening holes of your round, just as you will need to over the closing holes.

Cluster of bunkers guarding the right side of the green

**374YDS 342M
PAR 4**

For the third hole you turn through 90° and head eastwards. This is the first of three holes running in the same direction and the longest such stretch on the course. It is a medium-length par 4 which in some conditions could play quite long. The green is past a gap in a distant ridge (at 300 yards), and cannot quite be seen from the tee. Your driving line should be exactly on that gap, or a shade to the left of it, which would allow you to see a more generous slice of the green on your second shot. The driving zone is very generous, as much as 90 yards across in places, so I would expect the drive not to be a major problem for you. There is a bunker in the right rough at 160 yards, so hit well to the left of that and dismiss it.

Set into the hillocks or ridges on either side of the gap are quite substantial bunkers which might distract you. I would suggest that you try to eliminate them from your mind and concentrate on your target for the second shot, the green. This may require an extra effort, since you may not be able to see too much of it. The centre of the green is about 100 yards beyond that gap. The green, which is a huge rectangle, has two

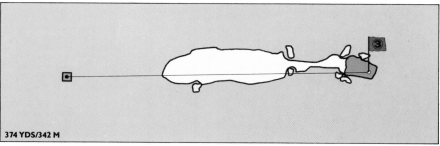

374 YDS/342 M

bunkers at the right-front corner, a bigger one at the left front, and another left centre, so it is quite strongly defended. You may not see any of these on your second shot, but there is a healthy, open frontage to the green and even if you are a shade off-line with your second, you have a reasonable chance of catching the putting surface, part-blind shot or no.

There are two important points to be made about this green, and therefore the shot to it. It is 44 yards long, and there is no trouble at the back. Thus there is a difference of four club-lengths from front to back, so you must be sure of your yardage. Walk forward by all means to check the pin position. If you are short, the ground from the gap to the green is flat and friendly, and you may be able to bobble the ball on. But the word here is long, not short. Take more than enough club if you are in any doubt. The green does go slightly uphill, which will help hold your shot. All told, a good par-4 hole which I rather like, but one which can play very differently from day to day depending on the conditions.

Left:
The generous driving zone in front of the ridge

Ridges hide greenside bunkers on the left and right

Gap at 300 yards with a deep bunker on either side

Approach to the 3rd

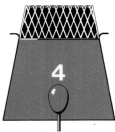

**174YDS 159M
PAR 3**

The first of Muirfield's short holes, the 4th, like the other three, is a rigorous test of your striking ability and accuracy with an iron club. All the same, let me tell you that this hole can play almost any length – I have used a driver here!

The green is built high – you will be hitting up to it – and is ferociously bunkered by fearsome traps; it falls off down very steep slopes on all sides. Even at the front there is a pronounced slope up to the putting surface, and this slopes up very positively from front to back, so if you are over the green, you will have to pitch back onto a slithery downslope.

The critical requirement with your tee shot is to pitch the ball on the putting surface. If you do that, or at least onto a reasonable part of it, you have a fair chance of staying on. I do not believe that this is an unfair hole, but I have no doubt that it is a very dangerous one, particularly when the wind blows.

There is one cross-bunker, about 100 yards out from the tee, and two bunkers just past it on the right, and another on the left front of the green. The rest of the green is unprotected, and a little bank rises above the right side towards the back of the green. But the bunkers are lethal. Any ball pitched just short, on the upslope to the green, perhaps even on the first few feet of the putting surface and not on a proper line, will be spun off and will run down wicked slopes into these traps. They are deeper than a tall man, with vertical revetted faces, and if you do get in there it can take you a lot of strokes to get out.

The green is 40 yards long, or three or four clubs' difference from front to back, and makes a severe test. Do not be too proud to take wood. You must consider the wind and weather conditions; you must take the right club; you must find the right line, which is slightly left of the centre front of the green, and you had better make sure you hit

The 4th

the shot well. If you score three here, be well pleased with yourself. I rate the hole at the very least as a par 3.5. I also have to tell you that Brian Barnes, in an Open Championship, actually scored one on the hole, so be of good cheer. I will not mention that Brian was so overcome by this that he scored seven on the next hole.

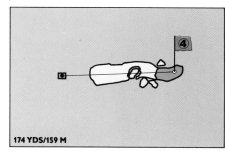

174 YDS/159 M

The yellow flags to the right mark the 12th and 13th greens

Green slopes up from front to back

Steep slopes and ferocious bunkers around the front of the green

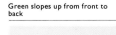

From the 4th Tee

506 YDS 462M
PAR 5

The 5th is the first of Muirfield's three par 5s, and all of them, I'm bound to say, are really great golf holes. This one keeps turning to the right throughout its length, and for that reason all the right side is firmly protected by strong rough and an outburst of bunkers, strategically placed. Into a hard wind, you might struggle just to reach the fairway – you must carry a good deal of broken ground and reach out a good 150 yards from the members' tee. That would leave you another 350 yards to cover, which sounds rather ridiculous. Yet for the average player, on a fairly still day, there is no reason to fear this hole. It can be a great pleasure, and very thrilling.

From about 150 to 250 yards, the right side of the fairway is closed off by five bunkers. There is one placed on the left, on the edge of the fairway at about 240 yards, with a smaller, supporting bunker 25 yards beyond it. The drive should be aimed exactly at that second bunker on the left, which will keep you out of all that débris on the right. From about 200 to 240 yards out, there is plenty of fairway; getting the ball in there will give you a good look forwards along and up the fairway. You must at all costs keep out of bunkers on this hole.

They are designed and placed at different ranges to catch long and short hitters alike, and there are 16 of them altogether.

Up ahead, you will see a cross-bunker coming in from the left. It is 100 yards from the front of the green, and it does narrow the fairway somewhat. It might therefore be 150 yards or more ahead of you, and you have to decide whether, under the conditions, you can carry it, or get past the right-hand end of it. If you do that, you will have an open shot at the green. But the 5th hole will not have finished with you. You then have to cope with a remarkable green.

It is fairly undulating, sloping down to the left, two-tiered, and with a slight ridge making the right side higher than the left. There are four bunkers all along the left side, from front left to back left, in general below the putting surface. On the right side of the fairway, 40 yards short of the green, is a bunker, backed by two more 30 yards behind it, only just in the right rough. And at the right centre, nudging into the putting surface, is the last of the traps, small, deep and sinister. After all that, please note that the ground just short, immediately in front of the green, will be likely to turn the ball from right to left, so that the open shot I spoke of may still be possible, but will require some extra care.

If you can bring this green within range of three shots, then I suggest that on the third

you concentrate on nothing but getting onto the green. Do not be tempted by the pin position. If it is tight to one side, play to the other side, or at least for the centre of the green. Do not be greedy with the pitch. Those green-side bunkers can undo all your good work.

In general, the hole is uphill all the way. That means your shots will fly a little higher, and cover less distance, with less run. If you are into a hard east wind, the 5th will seem endless. But, wind or no wind, if you go about the challenges of this hole rationally, you have a good chance of making par. And whatever you score, your compensation when you get there will be well worth it. You will have arrived at the highest

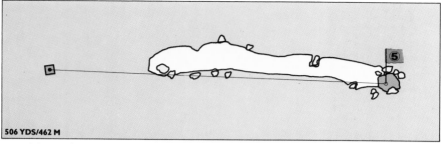

506 YDS/462 M

point of the Muirfield property and can rejoice in magnificent views of the Firth of Forth, Bass Rock and Berwick Law through the Lomonds of Fife and Gullane Hill and on up to the noble City of Edinburgh and the dramatic bridges beyond it. And again I must tell you, although you may well find it difficult to believe, that the American player, Johnny Miller, in the 1972 Open Championship, scored two on the hole. He used a driver and a 3-wood, and probably thought how simple it was, and wondered why he didn't do it every time he played the hole!

The fairway is liberally strewn with bunkers to left and right

Cross bunker 100 yards from the green

Go for the centre of the undulating green rather than risking greenside bunkers by attacking the pin

Approach to the 5th

436YDS 398M
PAR 4

The 6th is not an easy hole by any means, nor am I really sure what to say about it. In turn, I have the feeling that it is the weakest, the poorest, the strongest, the least fair of all the Muirfield holes. First time out, it really is quite difficult to know where to drive. You look up a rising fairway which has two bunkers eating in from the left. They are 212 yards from the back tee, and therefore driveable. These bunkers are clearly visible and virtually form the horizon, so to that extent, since you are driving 'at the sky', this is a blind drive. Officially

Stone wall is 116 yards from the front of the green

2nd shot at the 6th

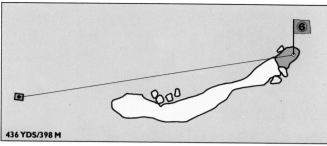

436 YDS/398 M

A view of the green showing the more generous entrance to the left

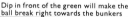

Dip in front of the green will make the ball break right towards the bunkers

Muirfield is proud of the fact that, unlike many other links courses, it has only one blind shot, the drive at the 11th, but I would be inclined also to rate this one a blind drive.

Immediately behind these two bunkers, completely out of sight but in close support, are two more; all are wicked, insidious traps, and so deep and with such high revetted faces that you may even have to play out backwards or sideways. Your line therefore must take you to the right of them, which will put you into a valley area from which the hole turns to the left. Just to complicate your life, if you drive too far into this valley, the ball will over-run the fairway into tangly rough.

From here you will still be a long shot, perhaps 200 yards, from the green. Level with the last of the four bunkers on the left, a path crosses the fairway, 175 yards from the front of the green. In addition, because of the folding ground, you will probably see very little of the putting surface, so put your faith in your yardage. You will see a stone wall, by the way, coming in from the left. The end of that wall, where it stops just short of the fairway, is 116 yards from the front of the green.

There are two big bunkers, one short right and the other at the right-front corner, with a smallish pot at the left centre. A dip in front of the green is deceptive. A ball pitching short and to the right will probably break into one or other of these bunkers, which are penal. If you are in there, and the pin position is set on the right of the green, you will have a horrible shot in prospect. I should aim slightly left of centre of the green on this second shot – the ball will tend to go right towards the centre. But I still think this is a rather cruel hole; if you make four here you have every right to feel ecstatic.

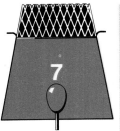

151YDS 138M
PAR 3

This hole runs to the west and so, if there is any wind prevailing, you will be playing directly into it; on such days the 7th becomes positively hostile. In its design and contouring it is probably not as extreme as the 4th (it is also 20 yards shorter), but with any kind of wind it can be very challenging. Of all Muirfield's four short holes, this is the only one which plays in a westerly direction, the others – 4th, 13th and 16th – running easterly, which you might judge a design fault, but all four are very demanding holes.

from the 7th tee

The 7th

The 7th, in common with the 13th, may be able to cope with a 'run-on' shot, but in general terms you should not be short at any of these holes.

The green is quite large, on a high plateau, so you will be hitting uphill all the way, as at all the short holes on this course. That in itself means you must think of 'one more club', as we say. The hole is closely trapped, one front right, one front left and two more up the left side, and off the back right and back left of the green there are quite brisk downslopes.

From the front of the front tee to the back of the back measures 68 yards and the green is 37 yards long, so your first exercise here is arithmetical – you must know exactly how far the tee in use measures to the flag. There is nothing beyond the green save a distant view of the Firth of Forth and the famous bridges, ancient rail and modern road, so there will be some lack of definition from the tee.

Finally, there seems to be a theory, put about by the Muirfield caddies, that the slope of this green is an optical illusion, and that there are no borrows on any putt. With the greatest respect to the local caddies, a magnificent body of men, don't believe it. There are borrows. I know. I have experienced them. This green is totally exposed, so the requirement here is nothing less than a fine assessment of the conditions, particularly of wind and weather, and your best strike at the ball, a first-class stroke which will get you the distance.

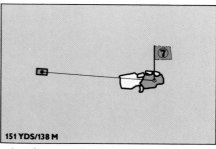

151 YDS/138 M

Left:
The line of bunkers waiting for the wayward tee shot

First of three bunkers along the left side of the green

Steep downslope behind the green

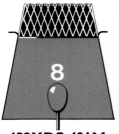

439YDS 401M
PAR 4

The drive must be aimed left
to avoid the mass of bunkers
from 200–260 yards

Of all the Muirfield holes, the par-4 8th illustrates perfectly the local philosophy of fairway bunkering in the driving zone, intended above all to lengthen the second shot, to funnel you towards the narrowest part of the fairway, and to reinforce the hole's Phase Two defences, ie those around the green or in play from the second shot. All this is as it should be, of course, if golf is to be more than a slugger's game, and points up the greatest single demand that Muirfield will make of you – for straight and accurate driving.

The 8th is a dog-leg turning to the right. In the angle, there are no fewer than nine bunkers, covering the range from 200 to 260 yards. There is no bunker on the left side of this hole, as well there might at around, for example, 250 yards. These nine traps look like an elephant's grave-yard, and they could certainly be your grave-yard if you get in there. Don't. Be well to the left of all of them. Be in the left rough if you have to – it is not too severe. If you are in these bunkers, you could tango from one to the other and use up three or four strokes to advance 50 yards.

Even if you drive nicely into the fairway, you will still not see the green. Two big cross-bunkers, set on a slight

From the angle of the Dog-leg at the 8th

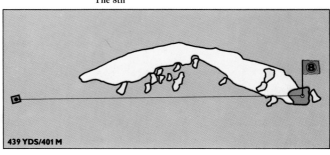

439 YDS/401 M

The area behind the cross-
bunkers and the solitary
bunker to the right of the
green

Cross-bunkers 50 yards from
the green

rise, with a third in the rough to the right, screen off everything but the top of the flagstick, and give the impression that the green is set in a bowl or a pronounced hollow. It is not. It is perfectly flat, and the approaches beyond the cross-bunkers are perfectly flat and fair. From the cross-bunkers to the centre of the green is a good 50 yards, so you have plenty of ground to work with beyond them. The thing to do on the second shot is ignore them and fly boldly over them.

You will then find that the green is virtually defenceless and that you have overcome the challenge of the hole. The green is wide, and of good length. There is one smallish bunker at the back left. The fringes and close approaches are all open and reasonably flat, so if you miss the putting surface you still have an honest chance for par with a chip and one putt. The major ramparts of the 8th are that scattering of heavy, forbidding traps in the dog-leg angle; if you skirt that lot, you have broken the back of the problem. The drive, as so often at Muirfield, is critical.

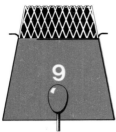

460YDS 420M
PAR 4

The 9th hole has been called an ancient monument, an antique, rubbish, a monster, coupled with a variety of unflattering adjectives, but I choose to think that it is a very fine par 5 from the championship tee, like the two others at Muirfield, and a great golf hole by any standards. It poses intriguing tactical problems, the first being that for medal, as opposed to championship, purposes, it is in fact a par 4, at 460 yards. Championship length is 495 yards and therefore a par 5. Please take my word that if the hole is played into any kind of west wind, no one will reach the green in two shots.

We find ourselves looking towards Grey-walls Hotel and the club-house of the Honourable Company of Edinburgh Golfers. A long, low greystone wall, an out-of-bounds wall, runs the entire length of the hole along the left. The first striking feature, critical to the playing of the hole, is Bunker A. This is a large cross-bunker coming into the left centre of the fairway some 200 yards from the medal tee. About 60 yards beyond it on the same line is another big bunker. The critical element here is that the rough comes into the fairway in front of Bunker A, continues back to embrace the more distant bunker and eliminates the entire left half of the fairway for a good 80 yards. The right half of the remaining fairway narrows to little more than 15 yards at one point.

In a sense, the decisions about your tee shot are simple. You must not be in Bunker A. You must not be left of it, and you must not be directly over it. You have two choices – either be short of it, and into a strong wind you may not in any case reach it, or you must be to the right of it. Don't be afraid of missing the fairway to the right. The rough, or at least the fringe rough, is not penal – you'll get a shot out of there. The whole thrust of the first part of this exercise really makes you play to the right. The problems set by the second shot mean that you are almost obliged to go left.

Bunker A is 230 yards from the front of the green. As you look forward, you will see a ridge running along the fairway; this leaves the left side, towards the wall, higher than the right. Along the edge of that lower right side is a line of four bunkers, 70 yards long, covering the line of a second shot that might be coming in from the right, or wide from the right.

These bunkers will gather in a shot not played positively towards the left side of the fair-way; to complicate that,

The view from the tee

2nd shot at the 9th

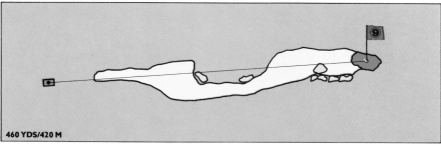

460 YDS/420 M

just past the nearest of them, and edging over towards the centre of the fairway, is the big Simpson's Bunker, named after the architect who put it there. So you are being steered left all the way on this shot, and of course that out-of-bounds wall up there is coming more and more into play. Good players have gone over it – Peter Thomson in an Open Championship, for one – but there is more space up there than you might think, or can see. On the second shot, you must get the ball up on that higher left side, towards the wall. I see no reason for you to crick your back going for length on this shot. If you can advance yourself, say, 150 yards from Bunker A, you will be level with or just short of Simpson's Bunker, and will have less than 100 yards to go to the flag-stick, and the best possible look at the green and the flag position.

For most average players, this will be a solid par 5 from the medal tee. Into wind, rate it 5.5. The more you try to be greedy and improve on these ratings, the more certain is the road to disaster on such a hole. There is no greenside bunker, but the green slopes from left to right. If the pin is on the left, or higher, side, you may find it difficult to pitch close. But if you have come this far this well, why not pitch on, take your two putts, score five, and walk off feeling like the Lord of Creation?

Out-of-bounds wall

Bunkers and rough narrow the fairway 220 yards from the tee

Bunkers line up below the ridge on the right side of the fairway

471 YDS 430M
PAR 4

The start of the second half at Muirfield, the counter-clockwise nine, is just as severe as the start of the front nine, and that opening hole. The 10th runs due north and the medal measurement of 471 yards is only five yards short of the par-5 distance. The hole runs due north in a straight line, and you may have difficulty in accepting that it is 11 yards longer than the 9th. The wisest course might be to play this one in five careful strokes. Over all the teeing grounds there is a 69-yard spread, so try to establish accurately which tee is in use and

the consequent yardage you are facing.

Again, fairway bunkers compromise the drive. There are two of them on the right side of the fairway. The first is some 240 yards from the back tee, the tee right back towards the stone wall, and the second is perhaps 30 yards further on. These are strong bunkers, so you must aim to the left of them. You will not see the green, only the flagstick, from the tee.

The prospect on the second shot is of a slight ridge across the fairway, still holding most of the green from view, with two cross-bunkers on it. This ridge is about 100 yards from the first fairway bunker, and the

Approach to the 10th

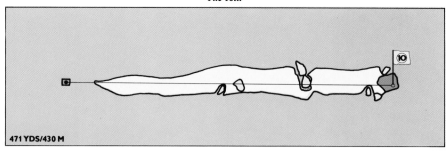

471 YDS/430 M

green is another 100 yards on. You may well be facing a lusty second shot of 180 or 200 yards, so you must try to ignore this cross-hazard and fly the ball over it. 'Easy to say,' I can hear you complain, but it has to be done. There is very little space, if any, to sneak past the outside ends of the ridge. Give yourself enough club, and give the shot your fullest and most positive swing. Do not be afraid of being too long – there is a ridge around the back of the green which will at least stop your ball. On the second shot, you will see a right-hand slice of the green, which is not too intimidating. The entrance is quite generous and it is not too tightly trapped. There are two bunkers short and slightly wide to the right, another closer to the green at the left centre. The green also helps by sloping up slightly towards the back.

Left:
A panoramic view of the fairway with the two bunkers on the right threatening the tee shot

Green slopes up at the back and a ridge helps to hold the approach shot

Ridge and cross-bunkers 100 yards from the green

350YDS 320M
PAR 4

Again we have a straight hole, another par 4 running in exactly the same northerly direction as the 10th, but it is a fairly short par 4 and not nearly so forbidding. At first sight you may not be inclined to agree with that, since the 11th is the classic blind-drive links hole, with a high ridge in front of the tee concealing every single scrap of fairway. The ridge looks formidable. You must not allow it to influence your thinking, or your swing, on the tee. From the very back championship tee it demands a carry of 195 yards, but from the very front of the front tee you are talking about 115 yards, an

altogether different matter. So probably what you do, as soon as you have out-stared the ridge, is check exactly which teeing ground is in use, establish the carry required, realize that it is not after all such a terror, and set about it.

Playing the hole for the first time, you would do well to hit directly over the marker-post, or if anything a shade left of it. When you have toiled over the hill, you will find a wide fairway area with good lies and stances. There is a bunker in the rough on the right at around 250–260 yards and another to the left of the fairway, 30 yards on. I don't believe either of these should trouble you, although if you are playing with a strong

Downslope and bunkers on the left

2nd shot at the 11th

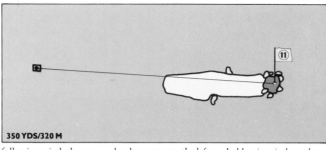

350 YDS/320 M

following wind, the one on the right might well be in range of your best shot.

Now that you have negotiated the ridge, you will see where the real defences of this hole lie – all around the green. An interesting green it is, too: clearly elevated, it has a dip in front which might take some of the yardage off your shot if it is a touch short. There is a slight tier effect across the green. The back portion slopes up quite noticeably, which will help hold the ball. The front of the green is fair, the entrance reasonably open and clearly designed to make the second shot a 'target' shot. Apart from the front, the green is ringed around with a garland of

bunkers, two on the left, three at the back (pressing in on the putting surface, on a downslope), and two at the right. These last two edge into the right-front corner, and give the impression of a spur of green, spreading away to the right, behind them. There is quite a lot of green in that area, and on high days and holidays you can be sure that the pin will be cut in there!

Given a drive taking you ten or twenty yards over the ridge, the average player should be playing a mid-iron or a pitching club, in still air, perhaps nothing much longer than a 6-iron. This should give you the height you need, and you should aim to pitch the ball on the front centre of the green. It should

hold quite nicely at the middle of a green which is 30 yards deep. There is one other point here, and it can be slightly discon-certing. The back of the green in fact forms the horizon, so in a sense you will be pitching up into an 'empty sky', rather like the drive on the 6th hole. But if you have the right club in your hand, do not be afraid of boldness on this second shot. The tendency for amateurs, I suspect, is to be short.

Left:
The ridge is a daunting prospect

Two bunkers cut into the front right of the green

Dip in front of the green

12

376YDS 344M
PAR 4

For the 12th you turn towards the south-west. It is slightly longer than the 11th, but looks altogether more friendly and sympathetic than most on the course. From a nicely built-up teeing area, we can see everything falling away quite pleasantly before us, all the way to the green. The strongest and most immediate feature from the tee is a ridge edging in towards the fairway to the left, with a big, forceful bunker at the end of it. This bunker is 230 yards out, and could well be your driving line, since the fairway, which up to that point is quite ample, slopes from left to right and will move a ball on that line in towards the centre. If you feel you can reach that bunker, drive to the right of it, but as close to it as you dare. There is a bunker just in the rough, on the right at 150 yards, and I certainly expect you to drive well past that. The rough on the right side of this hole, certainly the fringe rough, should not be all that punishing.

I would assess this as a fairly comfortable driving hole, but the second shot is rather interesting. The big bunker we have noted on the left side of the fairway, by the ridge, is in fact only 100 yards from the front edge of the green, but somehow the shot looks longer, more cramped, more

tricky than it should. I think the bunkering up the fairway and at the green is responsible for this sensation. The green is immediately protected, close up, by five bunkers. Since it is 40 yards long, quite open at both front and back, none of these bunkers really should be relevant to the second shot.

As so often at Muir-field, we have a pair of traps entering the fairway from the right, 40 yards short of the green, goodly-sized and side by side. If you have driven to the right side of the fairway, the line of your second shot may be directly over the inner of these two. There is another, ten yards further out, in the rough on the

Ridge and bunker on the left at 230 yards

2nd shot at the

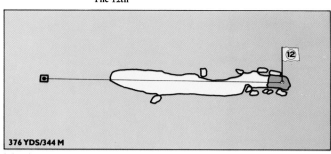

376 YDS/344 M

left. These are the traps which give the approach its rather cramped look.

In the area of the green, there is a bunker short and wide of the left-front corner, one halfway along the green on the left, a big one at the right back (these latter two are set in downslopes since this green is built up), and a pair placed tightly together just by the right-front corner. The green

The green and its right-side defences

is roughly rectangular in shape and is about 40 yards from front to back. It does slope off in minor fashion on the left side and at the back, but since it is built up and 'facing into' the shot, the ball should hold quite well. There is a slight dip and upslope at the front, but you could reasonably expect to run a ball on.

The task at the 12th is straightforward, given good 'management'. You

must get off a respectable drive into the fairway, without straining particularly for distance. You must then try to eliminate any illusions the bunkering might suggest; don't attempt to steer the ball but hit an honest pitch at the putting surface. Straight-forward golf holes require no more than straightforward golf shots.

Elevated green with downslopes all around

13

146YDS 133M
PAR 3

The 13th hole at Muirfield is, I believe, one of the world's greatest short holes. It also proves that greatness in a par-3 hole does not mean it has to be more than 200 yards long. It runs in an easterly direction, which offers up one of the few points of criticism of the Muirfield course, namely that three of the four short holes – the 4th and 16th are the others – run in the same approximate direction, and so most of the time they will be played downwind.

The green here is sited substantially above the teeing ground, and is set into a cleft in a high ridge. It is almost 50 yards long, but rather narrow, sloping upwards quite definitely at the front, then flattening out rather deceptively at the back, permitting a variety of wicked pin positions. Almost any pin position on this green can be wicked.

It is probably a platitude to say that on short holes you should ignore the bunkering, since the object of the exercise is to make the ball pitch on the putting surface, and stay there, as close to the flagstick as your shot-making talents allow; but bunkers are bunkers. They often have a hypnotic, magnetizing effect on the golfer. The bunkers on this hole are

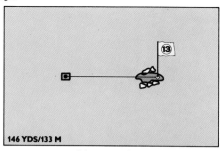

146 YDS/133 M

as diabolical as any that Muirfield can offer. There are two on the left side of the green, three on the right, all too close to the putting surface for comfort. These bunkers are set at the bottom of the sandhills which overlook the green on either side, and look more ominous and grasping because of it.

The bigger one on the left, very close to the putting surface, is more than six feet deep, with a vertical face. If you are plugged in there, you can send out for drinks and sandwiches – you may well be in there for the rest of the day. The problems of lie, stance, aim and elevation on the ball will be extreme.

I am not sure if there is a particular way to play this hole. You must know the correct range and have the right club and consider the playing conditions. Ultimately, though, the tee shot is a test of the golfer's courage and faith in his swing – courage at going

boldly for the flag, or at least the fat of the green. The only alternative is to be short and stammer the ball to the front of the green, which also means taking a chance on getting a first putt close. However, you may have 30 yards to go, and uphill!

Front-left bunker is more than 6 feet deep

The 13th green

Long narrow green sloping up from the front

The left-hand bunkers are barely visible from the tee

Three ominous bunkers on the right

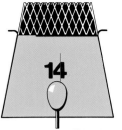

442YDS 403M
PAR 4

This is an attractive, open and unpretentious hole, with almost everything laid out nicely to be seen from the tee. The hole runs parallel with the 12th and is strikingly similar to it, although a good deal stronger and some 65 yards longer.

The landing area for the drive is really quite friendly in the 220–260 yard range, although it does rather narrow down beyond that. There is an enfilade of three bunkers in the left rough at these distances. On the right, level with the first of these, is a single bunker. The fairway breaks somewhat from

Above:
A wide area of fairway to the right of the three bunkers

Three bunkers protect the left side of the fairway at 220–260 yards

Fairway narrows and breaks from left to right

2nd shot at the

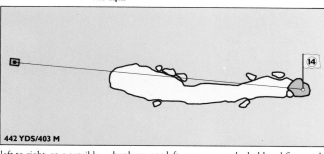

442 YDS/403 M

left to right, so a sensible driving line might be on the centre bunker (230 yards) of that left-hand set, with the ball pitching short and breaking to the right. A very good player might well carry past the first bracketing pair, and have the ball finish more or less level with the most distant bunker. For the average player, some care will be needed downwind – the nearest bunkers would certainly be reachable.

The second shot, depending of course on the drive, can be long, from 150 to 200 yards to the front of the green. Here we see what is becoming another Muirfield characteristic: a pair of bracketing

bunkers, one left, one right, each only just in the rough, about 80 yards from the centre of the green. There is one rather small bunker hard by the right-front corner of the green, another to the left, wide, and perhaps 20 yards from the green. Considering that you may well be playing a fairly long shot – you certainly will if you are into the wind – the green is not too large. The lie of the land suggests that you should come into this green from the left, where the entrance is open, and that is why most of the defences of the hole are along the left side. The back and left sides of the green are fairly clear.

Your second shot has

to be bold and firm, and pointed at the left centre of the green. This is a testing par 4 for the amateur player, and, into wind, a very strong hole for any class of player.

15

391 YDS 357M
PAR 4

Another fine par 4, the 15th is a good deal less intimidating than it looks from the tee. You may even find it almost recreational before you tackle Muirfield's powerful finish, which starts at the next hole.

This one is reasonably straight, and slightly downhill. A diagonal line of cross-bunkers stretching from 140–170 yards out should not cause problems unless there is a strong headwind. We will assume that you can carry them, and a good driving line would

be over the centre one. The fairway beyond is quite wide, slopes from left to right and 'onwards', and should be good for an extra 20 yards on your drive. I would say that this is one of the least demanding drives on the course.

The real test of the hole is concentrated on the second shot and this emerges not so much from the hazards you see as the impression they may make on you. A really good drive might put you about 150 yards from the green. Look up

the fairway and you will see, yet again, the Muirfield twins, bunkers on either side of the fairway about 60 yards short of the green. But this time, 20 yards on and smack in the centre of the fairway, is a third bunker, quite big. This

Green slopes away from the centre into bunkers on both sides

Approach to the 15th

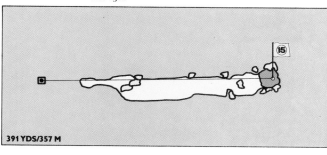

391 YDS/357 M

A fine view from the tee – the
Firth of Forth running inland
towards Edinburgh

may give you the feeling
that the entire area up
there is cramping and
narrowing. It isn't really.
The central bunker is the
culprit. It looks very
close to the green, but in
fact there is a good
30 yards of fair ground
between it and the front
of the putting surface.
You must carry this trap.
If you do, and your shot
is straight, you have a
fair chance of running on.

The green itself is
quite heavily trapped.
There are three bunkers
along the right side, a
small one rather wide of
the left-front corner, and
a very big bunker
covering all of the left
back. As you will see,
the front of the green is
quite open. However, it
is oddly contoured. The
left third falls off to the
left, the right third to the
right, and the central
third is flat but then
slopes upwards to the
back of the green.

The 15th is a
perfectly fair hole, one
which needs just a little
thought on the second
shot. Playing downwind,
take extra care that the
ball does not run away
from you, on both drive
and approach shot.

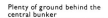

Plenty of ground behind the
central bunker

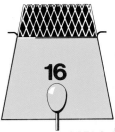

16

181YDS 165M
PAR 3

The last of Muirfield's short holes is the start of its ferocious finish. This is probably a good point in the round to realize that you have been playing a very big course, perhaps in strenuous weather which has made some physical demands on you, and that you may be tiring. So resolve to tackle this finish by playing within yourself, by keeping your swing in tight control, and above all by raising your concentration as many notches as you can.

You will certainly need all you can muster on the 16th. All the Muirfield short holes are difficult and challenging, this one – the longest – perhaps most of all. They all have much in common. All the greens are higher than the tees. All the greens are built-up and mounded. All the greens have sharp downslopes around them, and all these slopes feed awesome bunkering. All the greens are quite heavily defended, and finally all have some fierce contouring.

This hole has seven bunkers around the green area, and there used to be two more bunkers about 100 yards out, at the beginning of the 'fairway', if we can call it that. At this point, the ground goes down into a big dip or swale, rising again into the front part of the green. From the

tee, you can see only one greenside bunker towards the right-front corner, but in fact there are two there, with two more covering the right side and three curving around the left corner. The green is reasonably big, but has downslopes almost all the way around it. All these defending bunkers are very deep and penal, with very stiff faces.

You cannot expect to enjoy the luck of Lee Trevino in the 1972 Open Championship, when he exploded from one of these bunkers and saw his ball hit the flag-stick on the fly, and drop into the hole. If he had missed the stick, he might well have scored 5 on the hole. There is no alternative here but to (a) keep out of the

bunkers, (b) make sure you have enough club and (c) add one more club to be quite sure. Then – shoot for the back half of the green.

The danger zone is front right. If you are caught up in any of these slopes, your ball will be fed down into one bunker or the other. If the pin position is on the right, keep left. If it is on the left, keep right. Don't be too clever with this shot. Hit and hold the green. You will not make par easily – you will have to work very hard to score three on this hole – but then you are playing a great championship course, and you should not expect to get anything easily at Muirfield.

The 16th Green

The 16th

181 YDS/165 M

A large green but heavily defended

Back left is the safest landing area

Deep dip in front of fiercely contoured green

17
501YDS 458M
PAR 5

This is the last of Muirfield's great par-5 holes, and it may just be the best of them. It is a hole which in almost any conditions of weather poses very serious, but very exciting, problems on every shot. Into wind, for example, it will play very, very long.

Along the right side of the hole, all the way from tee to green, there are no man-made hazards whatsoever. At around 250 yards, the hole dog-legs to the left, and the temptation is to keep to the left, to reduce the distance. It is a temptation you must resist. In the angle of the dog-leg, stretching along for some 80 yards, is very broken ground and five bunkers. The first of that set of bunkers is 200 yards from the very back, championship tee, and you must at all costs drive to the right of it.

There is plenty of room on that side. Into wind from the medal tee (40 yards in front of the championship tee) you could reach that first bunker. Downwind you might reach the last one, so have a care. Play to the right – in fact from the tee you can see only the first of these bunkers.

When you get up to your drive, and you are neatly in the fairway and start shaping up to your second shot, you must immediately put on your

A wicked area of humps and hollows 100 yards from the green

Approach to the 17th

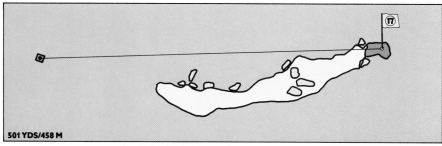

501 YDS/458 M

An intimidating view down the 17th fairway

tactical hat. The fact that this is a par 5 does not mean automatically that you will be reaching for a fairway wood, and blasting away. Governing your entire thinking on this second shot is an extraordinary stretch of ground. It covers the entire fairway and measures 30 yards or more from front to back; its centre is about 100 yards from the front of the green. It is an area of humps and hollows and slopes and ridges, and contains three of the biggest, most frightening of all Muirfield's bunkers. If you try to pass this area to the left, there is

a hostile bunker hidden just in the rough to snare you. You cannot pass it to the right – there is no fairway, and if you do go right, into the rough, you will have no practical third shot to the green.

You simply *must not* get into this area. It will totally destroy your score on the hole. You must either carry it, or stay short of it, and there is the challenge, and the nuisance, of the shot. Beyond this massive hazard is ample fairway area and a clean shot at the green. Short of it is ample fairway area and again a clean shot at the green, not much more than 140 yards away. If you are into a strong wind, and your drive has

been not too good, *think again*. Why not play an iron club that will keep you short of these bunkers, and leave another iron shot to the green? If you are down a strong wind (the hole runs with the prevailing wind at your back), and your drive has been quite good, ask yourself if you can carry that area comfortably. At all events you must take care because, whether you lay up short or carry over this zone, you must be on the left side of the fairway to get the best sight of the green. If the pin is on the right, and you are on the right after two shots, you have no shot on.

The green is long,

and has a flat entrance. There are bunkers on either side of the front, and banks along the left, back and right sides. Wind and weather conditions will govern your playing of this hole, but it is a thinker's hole, a planner's hole, a great golf hole. In 1966, Jack Nicklaus virtually won the Open Championship with the birdie he needed on the last round: downwind, he drove with a 3-iron, then hit the green with a 5-iron!

Three of Muirfield's biggest and most frightening bunkers

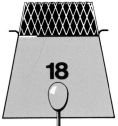

414 YDS 378M
PAR 4

Now you have arrived at the great climax to this exceptional golf course, and possibly the very best finishing hole of all our championship links. By that I mean, of course, the most difficult! I must say I would not feel particularly relaxed if I had to make 4 to win a Championship on this hole. It is straight, running almost due south, and is very sharply, very adroitly,

bunkered. The prevailing wind is right to left. There are problems on drive and second shot alike.

The fairway is narrow. There is a big bunker on the right, 190 yards from the medal tee. There are two bunkers on the other side of the fairway at 210 and 250 yards, and the gap between, equal to the width of the fairway, looks rather inhibiting. In fact, beyond these initial traps the fairway narrows and stays narrow. The drive must

find its way between these bunkers, or at least stay in the fairway, in their general area. A reasonably good player with a reasonably good drive should get past the one on the right, possibly level with or past the first of the two on the left. From there, he will be some 170 yards from the front of the green and about 190 yards from the flag. But to reach this green in two shots needs a very good drive indeed.

You had better not think that it is then simply a matter of

blasting away with your biggest gun – the second shot requires considera-tion. Up the fairway, a back-to-back pair of bunkers blocks out the left approach to the green. The bunkers are 40 and 20 yards short of the front respectively. The entire left side of the green is covered by one long bunker. The right side is covered by one almost as large, with a distinctive turf-covered 'island' in the middle. Thus if your drive has been good, you have to decide if you can carry

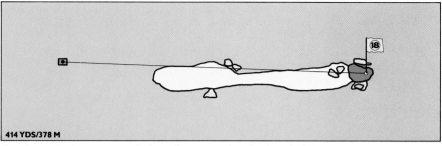

414 YDS/378 M

these fairway bunkers, a carry which may be all of 150 yards. There is a good 20 yards of true ground past that second one, which could help you run on. Your line then would be directly over the front of the two bunkers. If you think the carry is doubtful, then aim to the right, perhaps in line with the island bunker – but be short of it! Then you would have a short chip to the flag. The green, by the way, is slightly raised, and slopes up a little from the front.

Henry Cotton, in 1948, had two shots in that island bunker, scored five and still won the Championship. Gary Player in 1959 scored six on the hole, including three putts for a 68, and still won. Jack Nicklaus in 1966 used a 1-iron, then a 3-iron, to secure the par which won him the Open, while in 1972 Lee Trevino hit such a huge drive in the final round that his second shot was an 8-iron. In the last round of the 1980 Open Championship, I had a good drive down the left, and hit a 3-iron

three feet from the hole for a birdie. In front of that huge crowd in the 'stadium' around the last green, it was a very pleasing score. It jumped me up quite a few places in the prize-list, and at the same time I was sure that throughout the entire Championship there were more fives than fours scored on the hole. So play it, on your terms, as a par 4.5.

Left:
A view from the tee of one of the finest finishing holes in Championship golf

Bunkers blocking the left approach, but there is room behind them

Two bunkers to the left of the fairway at 210 and 250 yards

Approach to the 18th

Prestwick Golf Club virtually 'created' the Open Championship, and staged it for the first 12 years of its existence. By 1873, the Royal and Ancient club at St Andrews, and the Honourable Company of Edinburgh Golfers, then at Musselburgh, joined Prestwick, and the championship rotated around their three courses. By 1892, the Honourable Company had moved to its new course at Muirfield and was able to begin a sequence of marvellous championships played there since.

Course Record
63 Isao Aoki (Japan)
(Open Championship 1980)

Open Championship

1892 H H Hilton	305		1935 Alf Perry	283
1896 Harry Vardon	316		1948 Henry Cotton	284
1901 James Braid	309		1959 Gary Player (S Africa)	284
1906 James Braid	300		1966 Jack Nicklaus (USA)	282
1912 Ted Ray	295		1972 Lee Trevino (USA)	278
1929 Walter Hagen (USA)	292		1980 Tom Watson (USA)	271

Ryder Cup
1973 USA 16   GB 10
(Six matches halved)

Early winners of the Open Championship at Muirfield:
below, James Braid (1901, 1906); right, Harry Vardon (1896);
below right: Ted Ray (1912)

Amateur Championship

1897 A J T Allan	1926 J W Sweetser (USA)
1903 R Maxwell	1932 J de Forest
1909 R Maxwell	1954 D W Bachli (Australia)
1920 C J H Tolley	1974 T Homer

Walker Cup

1959 USA 9   GB 3   1979 USA 15   GB 8

(One match halved)

Home Internationals

1948 England   1956 Scotland   1976 Scotland

Curtis Cup

1952 GB 5   USA 4

Right: Walter Hagen putting on the 18th green in the final round of the 1929 Open. Below: Henry Cotton drives off the 10th in the 1929 Open watched by Walter Hagen. Nineteen years later, in 1948, Cotton himself was to become an Open Champion at Muirfield. Bottom left and right: Gary Player breaks down by the recorder's hut after taking 6 at the final hole in the last round of the 1959 Open, thinking he has let the title slip from him . . . but in the end he still finishes two strokes clear to take the trophy

Muirfield

Left: Jack Nicklaus playing out of a bunker at the 12th in the 1966 Open. Centre: Lee Trevino keeps talking and Tony Jacklin is on the receiving end during the 1972 Open. Below: Another long putt goes in for Trevino at the 9th

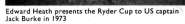

Edward Heath presents the Ryder Cup to US captain Jack Burke in 1973

The 1979 Walker Cup teams

Playing the course Muirfield, like Royal Troon, is the home of a private club, but the procedure for playing there is rather less intimidating than most people assume. You make arrangements in advance by obtaining an introduction from a member or by writing to the Secretary with an introduction from your own club's secretary. If practicable, a starting time will then be allocated. You will be warmly welcomed, and well instructed. Again contrary to general belief, ladies are permitted to play Muirfield provided they are accompanied in play by a gentleman. The clubhouse telephone number is Gullane (0620) 842123.

Recommended courses in the surrounding area There is no course immediately adjoining the Muirfield championship course but less than a mile away in the village of Gullane are the Gullane courses, numbers 1, 2 and 3, all delightful to play, rising and falling over Gullane Hill. Also within comfortable reach by car – a few miles – are Luffness New, Longniddry, Royal Musselburgh, Kilspindie, Dunbar and the famous and quite historic North Berwick.

Gullane GC, Gullane, East Lothian; tel Gullane (0620) 843115.

Luffness New GC, Aberlady, East Lothian; tel Gullane (0620 843114.

Longniddry GC, Longniddry, East Lothian; tel Longniddry (0875) 52141.

Royal Musselburgh GC, Prestongrange House, Prestonpans, East Lothian; tel Prestonpans (0875) 810276.

North Berwick GC, West Links, Beach Road, North Berwick, East Lothian; tel North Berwick (0620) 2135.

Kilspindie GC, Aberlady, East Lothian; tel Aberlady (08757) 216.

Dunbar GC, Dunbar, East Lothian; tel Dunbar (0368) 62317.

Where to stay Greywalls Hotel is literally on the course, by the 9th green and 10th tee. There are hotels and guest houses in Gullane itself, and a wider range of accommodation in neighbouring North Berwick.

Greywalls Hotel, Gullane, East Lothian; tel Gullane (0620) 842144.

Queen's Hotel, Main Street, Gullane, East Lothian; tel Gullane (0620) 842275.

Bisset's Hotel, Main Street, Gullane, East Lothian; tel Gullane (0620) 842230.

Dirleton Open Arms, Dirleton, East Lothian; tel Dirleton (062085) 241.

Marine Hotel, Cromwell Road, North Berwick, East Lothian; tel North Berwick (0620) 2406, telex 727363.

Right: Tom Watson on his way to the 1980 Open Championship
Below: Isao Aoki after breaking the course record

Muirfield